AF863541

Informed Separation

How to Prepare for a Good Divorce

Emily R. Sterling

© 2024, 2026 Emily R. Sterling

All rights reserved. The content contained within this book may not be reproduced, duplicated or transmitted without direct written permission from the author or the publisher.

ISBN: 978-1-923249-02-8 (e-book)

ISBN: 978-1-923249-03-5 (paperback)

Published by Elf Books. Cover design by Elf.

Disclaimer

This book is intended to provide general information and practical guidance for individuals considering or navigating separation and divorce. It is not intended to provide legal, financial, psychological, or other professional advice.

Divorce laws and procedures vary between states and jurisdictions, and individual circumstances differ. The information in this book should not be relied upon as a substitute for advice from a qualified professional who understands your particular situation.

The author and publisher have taken reasonable care in preparing this book but make no representations or guarantees about the accuracy, completeness, or suitability of its contents for any individual circumstances. Laws, procedures, and professional practices may change after publication.

Any examples or scenarios included in this book are illustrative and should not be taken as predictions of particular outcomes.

Readers are encouraged to seek appropriate professional advice before making decisions that may affect their legal rights, finances, personal safety, or family arrangements.

For anyone standing at the beginning of a separation, unsure of what comes next.

You don't have to have all the answers to take the next step.

Contents

Introduction

There is a difference between knowing that a marriage may be over and knowing what to do about it.

You might have been thinking about separation for months, or even years. You might have reached a decision only recently. Perhaps your spouse has made that decision for you. Whatever has brought you here, there are likely to be practical questions alongside the personal ones. Where will you live? What happens to the money? What should you tell the children? Who do you need to speak to, and what needs to happen first?

Some questions may have straightforward answers. Others will depend on information you do not yet have. You might find, for example, that the question of where to live cannot be answered until you understand your income and expenses, or that an arrangement that sounds sensible needs to be discussed with a lawyer before you act on it.

That is why preparation matters.

Informed Separation is about the things you can do to understand your circumstances before making decisions that may affect you and your family for years to come. It is not a promise that divorce will be easy or that careful planning will prevent disagreement. It is a way of approaching a difficult situation with more information, fewer assumptions, and a clearer sense of what needs your attention.

Preparation is not the same as having everything under control. You cannot decide how your spouse will respond, whether an agreement will be reached quickly, or how you will feel six months from now. You can, however, find out where important documents are kept, understand what money comes into the household, think about what your children need, and ask questions before making decisions that may be difficult to change.

Those ordinary steps can be easy to overlook when everything feels urgent. Yet they can make the next conversation, appointment, or decision considerably more useful.

What is a "good divorce"?

The subtitle of this book is How to Prepare for a Good Divorce. By "good," I do not mean cheerful, painless, or free of conflict. Nor do I mean that two people must remain friends or agree about everything.

I mean a separation handled as thoughtfully as circumstances allow: with attention to safety, fair dealing, the needs of children, and the practical realities of establishing two separate lives. For some couples, that may involve cooperative discussions and agreements. For others, direct conversations are difficult or unsafe, and a more structured process with professional support will be necessary.

A good decision is not necessarily the decision that keeps everyone happy. It is one made with an understanding of the available choices and their possible consequences. Sometimes the most constructive thing you can do is pause, get advice, and avoid making a commitment before you know what it means.

There will be moments when that approach is difficult to maintain. The aim is not perfection, but to make thoughtful decisions wherever circumstances allow.

What this book will help you do

We begin with the decision itself, including the uncertainty and mixed feelings that can accompany it. Then we look at getting legal advice early, making a practical plan, gathering documents, and understanding your financial position. These chapters are concerned with the information and arrangements that often need attention before, or soon after, a separation.

We then turn to the people involved: supporting your children, communicating with your spouse where it is safe and useful to do so, building a support network, and looking after yourself. The practical and personal parts of separation do not happen neatly one after another. They overlap. A housing decision may affect your children's routines. A difficult conversation may leave you too tired to think clearly about a financial question. That is normal, and it is one reason to approach the process in manageable pieces.

Throughout the book, you'll find examples, checklists, questions to consider, and simple exercises. Use whichever are relevant to your circumstances. They're intended to help you identify what you know, what information is missing, and where professional advice may be useful.

You do not have to read every chapter in order. If your immediate concern is money, start there. If you are worried about telling your children, turn to that chapter first. You can return to the other sections when you need them.

A word about professional advice and safety

Divorce and separation have legal and financial consequences. The rules that apply depend on where you live and your particular circumstances. This book does not explain the law in any individual US state, and it is not a substitute for advice from a qualified family law attorney, financial professional, or other appropriate adviser.

Getting advice early does not mean you have to start a court case or make a final decision that day. It can simply mean learning which choices are available, which deadlines or risks may matter, and which questions you should answer before taking the next step.

If there is abuse, intimidation, coercive control, or a concern about your safety or your children's safety, the usual suggestions about open communication and cooperation may not be appropriate. Do not feel obliged to announce plans or negotiate directly because a book encourages respectful discussion. Seek confidential, individualized support and advice about how to proceed safely.

Where to begin

You may have a notebook full of questions. You may have only one question, repeated over and over. You may be ready to act, or still working out whether separation is the right decision. There is room for all of those starting points here.

For now, consider writing down three things: what you know for certain, what you are assuming, and what you need to ask someone who can help. You might discover that a worry which feels enormous is really several smaller questions, each with a different answer. You might also discover that some matters need urgent attention while others can wait.

Begin with the facts you can establish and the advice you need. Some questions will require immediate attention. Others can wait until you have more information.

That is the work of an informed separation. And it is a useful place to start.

Chapter 1: Make the Decision

There is rarely a single moment when a marriage becomes difficult. More often, there are conversations you keep having, things you stop talking about, or a growing sense that the relationship is no longer working as it once did. Sometimes something happens that changes everything. Sometimes nothing dramatic happens at all.

You may have been considering separation for years, or the possibility may have appeared only recently. Either way, the question can sit alongside ordinary life. You still go to work, make dinner, collect the children, pay bills, and answer messages. Meanwhile, you are trying to decide whether the life you have built together can continue.

This chapter will not tell you whether to stay or leave. That is not a decision a book can make for you. Instead, we will look at the feelings that can accompany the decision, the circumstances that make one separation different from another, and ways to think clearly when there is a great deal to consider. The practical questions matter, but you do not have to answer them all before you begin thinking about what you want.

How Will You Feel?

Possibly several different things, sometimes in the same day.

You might be sad about what is ending and relieved that you have finally acknowledged it. You might be angry with your spouse and still care deeply about them. You might be certain about separating in the morning and full of doubt that evening. None of these feelings, on its own, tells you whether your decision is right or wrong.

There may be grief for things that have not happened yet: the holidays you expected to take, the home you imagined growing old in, or the family traditions that might change. You can grieve those possibilities even if the marriage has been unhappy for a long time. And you can miss the good parts of a relationship without deciding that you should remain in it.

Relief can be confusing, too. Perhaps you feel lighter when your spouse is away or when you imagine living separately. That feeling is worth noticing, but it is not a complete answer. Equally, fear about being alone or managing financially does not necessarily mean staying is right. Feelings provide information. They are not always instructions.

Try separating your emotional questions from your practical ones. "Will I be lonely?" is different from "Can I afford a place to live?" Both deserve attention, but they may call for different kinds of help. A trusted friend or counselor might help you talk through the first. A financial adviser or lawyer may help you understand the second.

You may also feel pressure to be certain. Friends may ask whether you have made up your mind; family members may want a reason they can understand. It is reasonable to say that you are still thinking. You can take the situation seriously without announcing a final decision before you are ready.

One useful exercise is to write down what you feel on an ordinary day, rather than only after an argument or a particularly good weekend. Over a few weeks, you may notice patterns. The aim is not to collect evidence against your spouse. It is to give yourself a more complete picture than the most recent conversation can provide.

It's Your Decision

Other people may have strong opinions about your marriage. Some will encourage you to leave. Others will urge you to keep trying. They may mean well, but they do not live inside your relationship.

You know things about your marriage that outsiders do not. You also have blind spots, as everyone does. That is why taking ownership of the decision and accepting support are not opposites. You can listen carefully to advice without allowing someone else to decide for you.

Start by asking what has brought you to this point. Was there a particular event, such as an affair, that changed how you see the relationship? Have the same problems continued despite repeated conversations? Have you stopped feeling heard or safe? Or have you and your spouse gradually developed different expectations of your shared life?

Then consider what you have tried. Some people have had frank conversations, sought counseling, or made changes that helped for a time. Others have not been able to discuss the problems openly. Not every marriage can or should be repaired, and seeking couples counseling is not appropriate in every situation, particularly where abuse or coercive control is present. You do not have to prove that you have exhausted every possible option before taking your concerns seriously.

It can help to distinguish between a change you hope your spouse will make and one they have actually made. A promise made during a difficult conversation may be sincere. What matters over time is whether behavior changes in ways that address the problem. Similarly, ask yourself whether the changes you are considering would be acceptable and sustainable for you, not merely enough to get through the next few weeks.

Here are some questions worth returning to:

- What is making me consider separation now?
- What would need to change for me to want to stay?
- Have I communicated those concerns, where it has been safe to do so?
- If nothing changed over the next year, how would I feel?
- What am I most afraid will happen if I leave? What am I afraid will happen if I stay?
- What information would help me make a more considered decision?

Your answers may reveal that you need more information, more time, or a conversation with a professional. They may also reveal that the decision itself is clearer than the practical questions that follow.

And remember that deciding to separate is not the same as having to decide every detail of the separation immediately. The legal, financial, housing, and parenting questions can be addressed in stages. Those questions are the subject of the chapters ahead.

Each Separation Is Different

Some couples reach the decision together. They may be disappointed that the marriage is ending but able to discuss how to tell the children, manage the home, and begin living separately. For others, one spouse has been thinking about leaving for a long time while the other is is tired of not knowing what kind of evening she and Lily will come home to.

When Stephanie imagines living separately, she feels relief. She also feels grief for the family life she wanted, anger about what has happened, and worry about money and where they might live. She still hopes Charlie will seek treatment. None of those feelings cancels out the others.

At first, Stephanie tells herself that she cannot make a decision until she feels completely sure. But certainty is not arriving. Some days Charlie is thoughtful and apologetic. On other days the same difficulties return. Stephanie begins to recognize that she needs to consider the pattern of their family life, not only the best or worst day.

She makes a private list of her immediate concerns. Is Lily safe? What would Stephanie need if she moved? Which documents and financial details could she gather appropriately? Who could provide practical support? What advice should she obtain before discussing her plans? Because safety may be an issue, she seeks confidential professional guidance rather than assuming that telling Charlie everything at once is the right approach.

Stephanie is not required to decide how she will feel about Charlie in six months. She can care about him, hope he receives help, and still consider whether living with him is workable for her and Lily. She also does not have to carry out the entire separation in a single week. Identifying the next safe, informed step is enough to begin.

Your circumstances may be nothing like Stephanie's. Perhaps you and your spouse are discussing separation calmly, or perhaps you are unsure whether you want to leave at all. The lesson is not that everyone should follow Stephanie's choices. It is that emotional uncertainty and practical preparation can exist side by side.

Before You Move Forward

If you are considering separation, try making three short lists. The first is what you know: the circumstances that have brought you here and what you have already tried. The second is what you do not yet know: perhaps where you would live, what your finances look like, or what arrangements could be made for the children. The third is who could help: a trusted person, a counselor, a lawyer, a financial adviser, or a specialist support service.

Keep these notes somewhere private if privacy is a concern, and avoid accessing accounts or documents you are not entitled to access. The point is not to build a case against your spouse. It is to make the decision less tangled by seeing which questions are emotional, which are practical, and which require professional advice.

You may decide to work on the marriage, to separate, or to gather more information before deciding. Whatever your circumstances, understanding the practical implications of your options can help.

That is where legal advice becomes useful. In the next chapter, we will look at when to seek it, what to ask, and how it can help you avoid decisions that may be difficult to undo.

Chapter 2: Get Legal Advice

Making an appointment with a family lawyer can feel like a bigger step than it is. You may be wondering whether you are ready to separate, worrying about the cost, or concerned that asking a legal question somehow commits you to ending your marriage. It does not.

A first appointment is a chance to find out what you need to know before making decisions that may be difficult to change. You can be uncertain about the relationship and still want to understand the practical implications of leaving. You can also be certain you want to separate and have no idea what happens next. Both are good reasons to ask for advice.

Divorce law is not the same everywhere in the United States. The procedures for ending a marriage, the rules affecting property and support, and the way parenting issues are addressed depend on the state and the circumstances. This book cannot tell you what a court would decide in your case, and it should not try. What it can do is help you make better use of the advice you receive.

In this chapter, we will look at when to make that first call, what you might need to ask, what the process could involve, and how to turn a legal conversation into a practical plan. You don't need to arrive knowing the law. You need to know what you want to ask.

Seek Legal Advice Early

It is usually easier to explore your options before you have made a significant change. Moving out of the family home, agreeing to a new arrangement for the children, transferring money, signing a document, or promising to pay a particular bill may have consequences you have not considered.

This does not mean you must wait for a lawyer before making every ordinary decision. It means recognizing when a decision is important enough to ask about first. If something feels urgent, tell the lawyer why. If a decision has already been made, explain that too. Advice is still useful after the fact, although some options may have changed.

Friends and family can be a wonderful source of support. They may also have strong opinions about what you should do. Perhaps someone tells you that leaving the house means losing it, or that a particular financial arrangement is always fair. Their experience may be sincere, but it is not a substitute for advice about your own circumstances. The details matter, and the law may be different where they live.

An early conversation may also help you avoid spending energy on the wrong question. You might be worrying about who will keep a particular item of furniture when the more pressing issue is how the mortgage will be paid next month. Or you may be focused on the formal divorce paperwork when you first need to understand the immediate arrangements for the children. A good adviser can help you sort what needs attention now from what can wait.

There is one important exception to the idea of taking your time. If you or your children may be unsafe, do not wait for a routine appointment to get help. Contact emergency services if there is immediate danger. A local domestic violence service may be able to help you plan safely, including how to seek advice without putting yourself at greater risk. Tell your lawyer about any threats, controlling behavior, or concerns about privacy so the advice takes those circumstances into account.

Choosing a Lawyer and Making the First Call

You are looking for someone who works regularly with family-law matters in the state relevant to your situation. A lawyer who handled a house purchase or a business contract for you may be excellent at that work without being the right person for a separation.

When you contact an office, it is reasonable to ask whether the lawyer handles matters like yours, what an initial consultation costs, how long it lasts, and whether you need to send information beforehand. Ask how future fees are charged and whether there are less costly ways to get advice on a limited question. Depending on your circumstances, legal aid organizations, court self-help services, or lawyer referral programs may also be worth exploring.

You should be able to ask questions without feeling foolish. If the explanation is full of unfamiliar terms, ask for plain language. If you feel rushed or cannot understand what the lawyer is recommending, say so. You are not expected to arrive with a legal vocabulary.

It is also sensible to think about communication. How will you contact the office? Who will answer routine questions? How quickly can you expect a response if something urgent happens? What information should you avoid sending through an email account or device your spouse can access? These practical details may matter just as much as how comfortable you feel in the first meeting.

A consultation is not a test you have to pass. You are deciding whether this professional can help you understand your situation and make informed choices.

Prepare for the Appointment

You do not need to bring a perfectly organized file. A short account of your circumstances and a few questions will be a good start. If you have documents readily and lawfully available to you, take them. If you do not, make a note of what is missing and ask what to do next.

A simple one-page summary might include when you married, whether you are already living separately, where each of you currently lives, whether you have children, and any immediate worries about housing, money, or safety. You can also note major assets and debts as you understand them. The information does not have to be exact at this stage; say when you are estimating.

Think about what you want from the appointment. Perhaps you want to know whether to move out, how to handle shared accounts, what arrangements to make for the children in the next few weeks, or how much the process may cost. Write your three most important questions at the top of the page. If you become upset or the conversation takes an unexpected direction, you will have something to come back to.

You may be tempted to tell the entire story of your marriage, beginning with the first argument. The history can matter, particularly where there are safety concerns or circumstances that affect legal advice. But a first appointment has limited time. Try starting with what is happening now, what you are considering, and what you need to decide. Your lawyer can ask for more background where it is relevant.

Do not access someone else's private accounts, guess passwords, secretly copy protected information, or take documents you are not entitled to access. If you are unsure what you may gather or retain, ask before doing it. Chapter 4 will return to documents in more detail.

Understand Your Legal Options

Legal advice is useful when it helps you understand the choices available to you, not when it simply gives you a long list of possible court proceedings.

Depending on your circumstances, you may need to discuss housing, parenting arrangements, financial support, assets and debts, insurance, or the formal steps for ending the marriage. You may need advice about one issue immediately and others later. Ask the lawyer to explain which questions are connected and which can be considered separately.

It helps to distinguish three things: what you would like to happen, what the law may allow or require, and what is realistically possible given the information available. Those three things will not always be identical. For example, you may want to remain in the family home. Whether that is practical may depend on finances, arrangements for children, agreements with your spouse, and legal considerations specific to your situation.

A lawyer may need financial records, information about your spouse's circumstances, or further details about the children before offering a clearer view. Ask what information would help them advise you more specifically and how you can obtain it.

If a lawyer suggests a course of action, ask what problem it is intended to solve. What are the benefits? What are the risks? What might it cost? What would happen if you waited? And what would change the advice? Understanding the reason behind a recommendation makes it easier to decide whether it fits your circumstances.

What Might the Process Involve?

People often speak about "the divorce" as though it were one event. In practice, several different questions may need attention: how a marriage is formally ended, what happens to property and debts, what financial support may be relevant, and how children will be cared for. The legal relationship between these issues depends on where you live

Some people reach agreements about many practical matters before filing anything with a court. Others need formal orders or assistance with an urgent problem. There may be discussions between lawyers, an exchange of financial information, mediation, another form of dispute resolution, or court proceedings. Not every case follows all of these steps, and they do not always happen in a neat order.

Financial information is often an important part of the process. You may be asked to provide records of income, accounts, assets, and debts. In some situations, a professional valuation of a home, business, or other asset may be needed. If children are involved, the questions may include routines, school, healthcare, communication, and safety. More specialized assistance may be appropriate in some cases, but it should not be assumed that every family needs an assessment or a court hearing.

Mediation or negotiated discussions can be useful when people have enough information and can participate safely and meaningfully. They are not suitable in every situation. If there has been intimidation, coercive control, or violence, explain that before agreeing to any process. Ask what safeguards or alternatives exist.

Where agreement cannot be reached, a court may be asked to decide particular issues. That does not mean you have failed, and it does not necessarily mean every issue will be contested. The important thing is to understand the options relevant to your circumstances rather than imagining a single inevitable route.

Ask your lawyer to draw a simple outline of what the next few months might look like. Which steps are likely? Which are only possibilities? Are there deadlines? What information will you need? Where might costs arise? A sketch on a page can be easier to use than a long explanation remembered imperfectly after the meeting.

Develop a Practical Strategy

The word "strategy" sometimes makes divorce sound like a contest with a winner and a loser. That is not how I am using it here. A strategy is simply a considered approach to the decisions ahead.

Start with what matters most. You may be concerned about the children's routines, having somewhere affordable to live, keeping access to important records, or making sure a particular debt does not grow. Write those concerns down. Then separate what you know from what you are assuming. "I cannot afford the house on my income" is a question to test with actual numbers; "I will definitely lose the house" may be a fear rather than a fact.

Next, think about timing. Some matters need prompt attention, while others benefit from waiting until you have more information. It may be sensible to gather financial records before discussing a proposed settlement. It may be necessary to arrange immediate living expenses before considering longer-term property questions. Ask your lawyer which steps should come first.

A strategy also means knowing where you have flexibility. You might prefer one arrangement but be willing to consider another if it meets your essential needs. There may also be boundaries you cannot reasonably compromise, particularly around safety. Being clear about those distinctions can help you avoid arguing over details that do not matter while overlooking something that does.

Finally, allow the plan to change. New information may emerge. Your spouse may respond differently than you expected. A child may need additional support. A plan is useful because it gives you a place to start, not because it predicts every development.

Peta and Frankie

Peta and Frankie have decided to separate. They do not have children, but their financial circumstances are complicated. Peta owned substantial assets before the marriage, and she is worried that separating will put everything she brought into the relationship at risk.

Peta has already formed a view about what should happen. She believes those assets ought to remain hers. Frankie sees the finances differently. Their early conversations go in circles because each is arguing from a position they feel strongly about, without knowing which facts or legal considerations may be important.

Peta makes an appointment with a family lawyer. Beforehand, she writes down what she owned before the marriage, what has changed since, and which records she can find. She also prepares a basic estimate of her current expenses. The lawyer asks questions Peta had not considered: about how particular assets have been used, what records exist, and what information may be needed to assess the situation under the law that applies.

The lawyer does not promise that Peta will keep everything she owned before the marriage. Nor do they tell her to give up her concerns. They explain why more information is needed and discuss ways to approach the financial issues without making assumptions about the result.

Peta leaves with a short list. She will collect the documents she is entitled to access, work out what it costs her to live each month, and return for further advice before making an offer. She also decides not to continue arguing with Frankie about the same question every evening. Until she knows more, those conversations are not getting either of them anywhere.

Peta's situation is only an example; it does not tell you how premarital property would be treated in your state. What it illustrates is the difference between having a strongly held position and having an informed plan. Peta still does not know the outcome. She does know what she needs to find out next.

Questions Worth Taking with You

You may find it useful to take the following questions to an initial consultation. Choose the ones that fit your circumstances rather than trying to work through them all.

- What should I understand before making any changes to our living arrangements?
- Are there urgent steps or deadlines that apply to my circumstances?
- What should I do about shared accounts, bills, debts, and insurance while we work things out?

- If we have children, what immediate arrangements should we consider, and what should I avoid assuming?
- Which documents should I gather, and how can I do that lawfully and safely?
- What options might be available for discussing an agreement without going to court?
- What would make direct negotiation or mediation inappropriate in my situation?
- What is likely to happen next, and what could change that sequence?
- How are your fees charged, and what can I do to use your time efficiently?
- What should I do if my spouse takes an unexpected step or something becomes urgent?

You do not have to leave with answers to every question. A good appointment may reveal new questions. Make a note of them rather than trying to hold everything in your head.

After the Appointment

When you get home, take ten minutes to review your notes while the conversation is fresh. Put the tasks into three groups: things to do soon, things to gather or check, and things that can wait. If you did not understand something, contact the office and ask for clarification. It is better to ask than to act on a guess.

You might also notice how you feel afterwards. Some people feel relieved to have information. Others feel unsettled because the situation has become more concrete. Neither reaction tells you whether you are making the right decision. You have simply learned more about what may be involved.

You are still responsible for choosing how to proceed, with advice appropriate to your circumstances. You do not have to make every decision in the first meeting, and you do not have to agree to a course of action you do not understand.

Before you put your notes away, identify the decisions that need attention first and the information you still need to gather. Those two things will form the beginning of your practical plan.

In the next chapter, we will look at how to turn that information into arrangements for the weeks ahead, including housing, expenses, and everyday responsibilities.

Chapter 3: Have a Plan

Once you have decided to separate, practical questions have a way of arriving together. Where will you live? How will you pay the bills? What will happen with the children? Should you tell your family now, or wait until you have something definite to say? And which decisions need to be made this week rather than next month?

It can feel as though you are expected to produce an entire new life plan at the very moment you have the least energy to make one. You are not. A useful separation plan begins with the next few days and weeks. It gives you somewhere to put the questions, rather than requiring you to carry them all around in your head.

Your plan may change. You might learn something about the finances, discover that a housing option is unavailable, or realize that a proposed arrangement does not work for your children. Changing a plan in response to new information is not a failure. It is what plans are for.

This chapter looks at immediate priorities, housing, living separately under one roof, and the small decisions that can make a difficult transition more manageable. The aim is not a perfect separation. It is a thoughtful starting point.

The Importance of Having a Plan

Start by separating what is urgent from what is important. You may have several important questions about property, finances, and parenting, but not all of them require an answer today. The immediate questions are often simpler: Is everyone safe? Does everyone have somewhere to sleep? Can the essential bills be paid? Do the children know who is collecting them from school?

A plan is particularly important when there are safety concerns. If you are frightened of your spouse, have experienced threats or controlling behavior, or believe that announcing a separation may place you or your children at risk, do not treat this chapter as a checklist for a joint conversation. Seek confidential assistance from a domestic violence service, a lawyer, or another appropriately qualified professional before discussing plans or changing arrangements. A specialist can help you think through safe communication, access to money, documents, transportation, and accommodation. If there is immediate danger, contact emergency services.

Even where there is no violence, separation may not be a situation in which both people can plan calmly together. One person may have spent months thinking about leaving while the other has only just heard the news. You may agree on some immediate matters and disagree about everything else. Your first plan can be yours alone: a list of what needs attention, what you need to find out, and who might help.

It can help to divide your plan into three time frames. First, the next 72 hours: safety, sleeping arrangements, medications, meals, work, childcare, and any pressing expenses. Second, the next few weeks: housing costs, a legal appointment, access to records, a workable routine, and support. Third, the longer term: decisions about property, formal arrangements for children, and the future financial picture.

Start with what needs attention now. The longer-term questions can wait until you have more information.

Keep the plan somewhere private and secure, particularly if another person has access to your devices or accounts. It does not need to be beautifully formatted. A notebook, a document, or a few lines written after an appointment will do. The value lies in being able to return to it when your thoughts are crowded.

Where Are You Going to Live?

Housing is often the most immediate practical difficulty. Two households generally cost more than one, and a home is rarely just a financial decision. It may be where your children feel settled, where your work is nearby, or where you expected to spend the next twenty years.

You might want to stay in the family home but be unsure whether you can afford it. You might want to leave but have no obvious place to go. You might both want to stay. Or you might agree that one person will move out, only to discover that finding a rental is harder than either of you expected.

Begin by considering short-term possibilities without assuming they must become permanent. Could you stay with a trusted friend or family member? Is temporary accommodation affordable and available? Could one of you remain in the home while the other looks for somewhere else? Would sharing the home for a limited period be safe and realistic? If you have children, consider school, childcare, transportation, activities, and the ordinary routines that help their days feel familiar.

Write down the actual cost of each option. Rent is only the beginning. There may be a security deposit, utility connections, moving costs, furniture, additional transportation, and expenses associated with running two homes. If you are staying with someone temporarily, ask what the arrangement would involve and how long it could reasonably last. A generous offer can still have limits.

Do not assume that moving out settles who owns the home or what will happen to it. Nor should you assume that remaining there guarantees any particular outcome. The legal and financial implications depend on your circumstances and where you live. Before making significant decisions about a mortgage, lease, jointly owned property, or arrangements involving children, get advice from a qualified local professional. If safety requires an immediate move, seek urgent assistance rather than waiting for an ordinary appointment.

You may also need to distinguish between what you want emotionally and what is workable practically. Staying in a home filled with memories may be comforting for one person and exhausting for another. Leaving may bring relief but create financial pressure. Neither response tells you what the right decision must be. It tells you which considerations deserve attention.

Try asking yourself: Where could I realistically live for the next month? What would that cost? What would I need to take? What would make the arrangement difficult? And which parts of the decision should I discuss with my lawyer or financial adviser before committing?

Separation Under One Roof

Some couples continue to live together after they have decided to separate. This may be a deliberate temporary arrangement or the only affordable option for the moment. Housing shortages, childcare, work schedules, health needs, and uncertainty can all make separate homes difficult to arrange quickly.

Living under one roof after separation is not automatically a mistake. It is also not automatically a sensible way to save money. What matters is whether the arrangement is safe, workable, and tolerable for the people involved.

The emotional mismatch can be considerable. One person may feel relieved that a decision has finally been made; the other may still be hoping the marriage can be repaired. One might want to discuss bills and schedules over dinner, while the other can barely sit at the same table. Everyday tasks such as grocery shopping or deciding who uses the car may suddenly carry more meaning than they used to.

If you are considering this arrangement, think about the practical boundaries. Where will each person sleep? Which spaces are private? How will household costs be paid? What is an appropriate time to discuss practical matters? Can either person invite visitors into the home? What will you tell the children, and how will you avoid drawing them into adult disagreements? If you share devices, accounts, or calendars, consider whether your privacy arrangements need attention.

You do not have to turn the home into a set of formal rules, but vague assumptions can create unnecessary friction. It may help to agree on a few clear expectations and review them after a short period. If discussing boundaries leads to repeated arguments, consider whether a neutral professional could assist, provided that doing so is safe and appropriate.

Children may notice changes in the atmosphere even when parents believe they are hiding their difficulties. That does not mean sharing a home will inevitably harm them. It does mean that adults should pay attention to conflict, tension, routines, and what children are being asked to manage. A child should not have to carry messages, monitor a parent's mood, or decide which parent is right.

If there is intimidation, coercion, escalating conflict, or fear, better household rules are not a substitute for a safety plan. Seek specialist support and advice about alternatives. You do not owe anyone continued cohabitation to prove that you are being cooperative.

Where living together is manageable, set a date to review it. Ask what would need to change for one or both of you to move, and what information you still need. A temporary arrangement can be useful without becoming an indefinite one.

Plan for a Smoother Transition

Consider Lucy and Heath. Heath told Lucy that he wanted to end their marriage. Lucy had not expected the conversation and was devastated. Heath had been thinking about separation for some time and was ready to talk about logistics. Lucy was still trying to understand what had happened.

They initially decided to remain in the family home while they worked things out. It seemed sensible. Neither would have to find accommodation immediately, the children could keep their routines, and the usual bills could continue to be paid. They told themselves it would only be for a little while.

The difficulties appeared in ordinary moments. Heath wanted to discuss a possible rental property while Lucy was making dinner. Lucy asked questions about whether the marriage could be saved when Heath believed they had already settled that issue. They were both tired. Conversations that began with school pickup times ended with hurt feelings about the relationship.

After several difficult weeks, they recognized that the arrangement was not giving either of them much room. Heath explored temporary accommodation and worked out what it would cost. Before making changes, they sought advice about their immediate financial and parenting questions. They then agreed that Heath would move out for the time being and Lucy would remain in the home with the children while they considered longer-term options.

They made a short list of the bills due over the following month and how those would be managed temporarily. They agreed on a predictable way to discuss the children's schedules, rather than raising questions whenever one of them walked into the kitchen. They also identified which decisions required further professional advice and resisted the temptation to settle everything in one conversation.

Moving out did not resolve the property questions or determine their future parenting arrangements. Lucy still had difficult days. Heath still had practical worries. But they were no longer trying to manage every part of the separation in the same rooms where they were struggling with the end of the marriage.

Lucy and Heath's arrangement will not suit every family. Moving out may be unaffordable, while remaining together may be manageable for some couples. Where violence or coercion is present, safety must come before cooperation.

Their experience illustrates an important distinction: an arrangement can work for now without being the right arrangement indefinitely.

A Practical Starting Plan

If you are unsure where to begin, try making a plan for the next two weeks rather than the next two years. Use the questions below as prompts, not a test you must complete.

Safety. Is anyone at risk? Do I need confidential advice before making a change or telling someone about my plans? Who could I contact in an emergency?

Housing. Where can each person stay in the immediate future? What are the likely costs? Is any arrangement temporary, and when should it be reviewed?

Children. Which daily routines need to continue? Who will handle school, childcare, medical appointments, and transportation over the next fortnight? What should the children be told in an age-appropriate way?

Money. Which bills are due soon? What income and funds are available for essential expenses? Which accounts or commitments do I need to understand before acting?

Advice. Which decisions might have legal or financial consequences? What are my three most important questions for a lawyer or other professional?

Support. Who can help with something specific: a school pickup, a place to stay, a meal, or simply listening without taking over?

Next action. Choose one manageable task. It might be booking an appointment, listing household expenses, checking a housing option, or arranging help with childcare. Give it a realistic date. If you cannot complete it, work out what information or support is missing.

You can keep a second list headed "Not for today." Put the longer-term questions there. You are not ignoring them; you are deciding that they do not all deserve your attention at the same time.

Before You Move On

A useful plan helps you distinguish between what needs attention now and what can wait. Begin with safety, housing, essential expenses, and the routines that need to continue. Record the questions you cannot yet answer and seek advice before making significant commitments.

As circumstances change, return to your plan and adjust it.

In the next chapter, we will look at the documents worth gathering so that, when you do ask for advice or consider your options, you have reliable information to work with.

Chapter 4: Gather Documents

Paperwork is rarely anyone's favorite part of separation. It may feel especially unappealing when you are trying to work out where to live, how to speak to your spouse, or what to tell the children. Yet collecting documents is one of the more useful things you can do while other decisions remain uncertain.

You do not need to understand every account, find every missing statement, or build an elaborate filing system. The aim is simpler: begin putting together a reliable picture of your circumstances. A document can answer a question that otherwise depends on memory. Sometimes it raises a question you did not know to ask. Both are useful.

If you have usually managed the family finances, you may already know where most of the information is kept. If your spouse has handled them, the task may feel more difficult. That does not mean you have failed to prepare. Start with the information you can safely and lawfully access, and make a list of what you do not have. Your lawyer can advise you about obtaining other records appropriately.

Why the Documents Matter

Imagine trying to explain your household finances from memory. You might remember roughly what you owe on the mortgage, but not the interest rate or whether the balance has changed. You may know that your spouse has a retirement account, but not its value. Perhaps you remember a loan being paid off, only to find there is still a balance outstanding.

Statements, agreements, and records give those conversations a firmer starting point. They help you and your advisers distinguish what you know from what you think you know. They may also make meetings more productive. Rather than spending the appointment trying to reconstruct a list of accounts, you can use the time to discuss the questions the records reveal.

Some documents matter because they show what exists now: account balances, debts, income, and regular expenses. Others help explain how something came about. Records relating to a gift, inheritance, business, or property owned before marriage may be relevant to questions your lawyer will consider. Their significance depends on your circumstances and the law where you live; you do not need to decide that yourself.

Documents are not a guarantee of a quick or agreeable divorce. They cannot make someone cooperate, and they will not resolve every disagreement. They can, however, reduce avoidable confusion and help you respond when information is requested.

Start with What You Can Access

Before downloading anything, consider where the records are and whether accessing them is appropriate. There is a difference between obtaining a statement from an account you are entitled to use and entering someone else's private account without permission. Do not guess passwords, use another person's login, or copy private material simply because you think it could be relevant.

If your spouse controls the documents, make a note of what is missing. You might know that a retirement account exists without having a recent statement, or that your spouse owns a business without having seen its tax returns. Record what you know and ask your lawyer how the remaining information can be obtained.

Safety matters as well. In a controlling or abusive relationship, searching for records, opening a new account, or using a shared computer could be noticed. If you are concerned about monitoring or retaliation, speak with a lawyer or an appropriate support service about a safe approach before taking action. The paperwork can wait until you know how to handle it safely.

A Checklist to Get You Started

This is a working list, not a test. Some categories will not apply to you. You may already have several items, and others may take time to obtain. Your lawyer may ask for additional information depending on your situation and the process involved.

Financial records

- Statements for checking, savings, and investment accounts, including joint accounts
- Recent personal, joint, or business tax returns, where available
- Pay stubs, employment records, and evidence of other income
- Retirement and pension statements, including 401(k) and IRA accounts
- Mortgage statements and documents relating to other property loans
- Credit card, car loan, student loan, and personal loan statements
- Household budgets and records of regular expenses

Legal and personal records

- Marriage certificate and any earlier divorce decree
- Prenuptial or postnuptial agreements, if applicable
- Existing separation agreements or court orders
- Wills, trusts, and powers of attorney
- Identification documents, including passports and Social Security information, stored securely

Property, business, and insurance

- Real estate deeds and any available valuations
- Vehicle titles and registration documents
- Records of valuable personal property, including available appraisals
- Documents relating to gifts, inheritances, or property owned before marriage
- Business ownership records and financial statements, if relevant and available to you
- Homeowners, renters, vehicle, health, and life insurance policies

Children and ongoing arrangements

- Children's birth certificates
- Existing parenting plans, custody orders, and support agreements

- Relevant school and health information, where appropriate
- Records of childcare, education, health, and other regular child-related expenses

You do not need to obtain every school report or medical record simply because children are involved. Collect what is relevant and ask your lawyer what else may be needed. Sensitive information about children deserves particular care.

Make a System You Can Actually Use

There is no prize for the most beautiful set of folders. A basic paper binder, a few clearly named digital folders, or a combination of the two will do. The best system is one you can return to without wondering where everything went.

You might create folders called Banking, Income and Tax, Property and Debts, Retirement, Insurance, and Children. Within each folder, use names that identify the document and its date: "Joint checking – June 2026," for example, rather than "statement final 2." Keep the original document where possible and avoid changing figures or writing over records.

If you have a pile of paper, sort it by category first. You can put the contents in date order later. If you have dozens of downloaded files, start by renaming the most recent ones. Do not let the organization become a project so large that you never get to the information itself.

Think carefully about where you store records. A shared cloud account, family computer, or email address may not be private. Use appropriate password protection and a secure location, particularly for identification documents and financial details. If you are unsure whether a device or account is monitored, get safety advice rather than experimenting.

A simple tracking sheet can help. Make four columns: Document; What I have; What is missing; Questions. You could write “Mortgage statement” in the first column, “March statement” in the second, “Current balance” in the third, and “Is the loan fixed-rate?” in the fourth. The point is not to answer every question immediately. It is to make sure the question does not disappear.

When the Documents Tell You Something Unexpected

Gathering records can be surprisingly emotional. You may find an account you had forgotten about, a debt you did not know existed, or a reminder of plans you made together. Even an ordinary bank statement can bring back memories of a different time.

Try to separate the immediate emotional response from the practical task. If you notice a transaction you do not recognize, record the date and amount. If a loan balance surprises you, note it and keep the statement. You do not need to confront your spouse or draw conclusions from one entry. There may be an explanation, and your lawyer or financial adviser can help you decide what requires further investigation.

The same applies if you suspect information is missing or inaccurate. Preserve what you already have and seek advice. Avoid trying to investigate by accessing accounts or devices you are not authorized to use.

Being Open About Information

Financial disclosure is often part of the divorce process, but the requirements, timing, and methods differ by state and by the procedure being used. Your lawyer can explain what information you are required to provide and how it should be exchanged.

It is important not to hide, destroy, alter, or selectively omit relevant records because you think they may be unhelpful. Incomplete or inaccurate information can create serious problems. At the same time, being open does not mean sending every sensitive document directly to your spouse without guidance. There may be appropriate ways to share information through lawyers, mediation, or formal processes, particularly when communication is difficult or unsafe.

It may help to think of gathering and disclosing as two separate steps. First, identify and organize the information. Then obtain advice about what needs to be shared, with whom, and when. That distinction allows you to be thorough without acting hastily.

Preparing for Your Next Appointment

You do not have to arrive at your lawyer's office with a perfectly complete folder. A useful starting package might include a recent tax return, available account and debt statements, a list of major assets, and copies of any existing agreements or orders. Bring your list of missing documents too.

Before the appointment, write down the questions that matter most. Which documents should you prioritize? Are there records you should preserve now? What information will be needed about a business or retirement account? How should you obtain documents that are not accessible to you? What are the safest arrangements for exchanging information?

If professional fees are a concern, ask whether there is a preferred way to label or send records. Organized information may save time, but only if it is organized in a way your adviser can use. Do not spend hours scanning every page before checking what is actually needed.

A Practical Exercise: Twenty Minutes at a Time

Choose one category from the checklist. Set aside twenty minutes to locate what you already have, download statements you can access appropriately, or write down what you need to request. At the end of that time, make a note of the next step and stop if you need to.

For example, you might begin with bank accounts. On the first day, list the accounts you know about. On the second, save the latest available statements. On the third, identify any missing information and add it to your questions for the lawyer.

After three short sessions, you have a useful starting point without having spent an entire weekend on paperwork.

If there is a deadline or an urgent safety concern, your priorities may be different. Follow professional advice about what needs immediate attention. Otherwise, small, consistent efforts are usually more manageable than trying to do everything in a single weekend.

The documents are a starting point. They show what you can establish from the records and help you identify what still needs explaining.

In the next chapter, we'll use that information to look more closely at your finances: income, expenses, assets, and debts.

Chapter 5: Understand the Money

Money can make separation feel suddenly real. A conversation about ending a marriage may be difficult enough; working out how to pay for two homes can make it harder still. There may have been two incomes supporting one household, or one person may have earned most of the money while the other managed the home and children. Either way, the arrangements that worked before may no longer work in the same way.

Begin by building a reasonably accurate picture of your finances: what comes in, what goes out, what you own, and what you owe. Some figures will be straightforward. Others may need to be estimated or confirmed.

The aim of this chapter is not to turn you into a financial expert. It is to help you ask better questions, prepare for professional advice, and avoid making important decisions on the basis of guesses.

Why the Financial Picture Changes

One household becoming two usually brings additional costs. Someone may need a rental deposit, furniture, moving expenses, or a second set of utilities. Childcare and transportation arrangements may change. Health insurance or other benefits may need attention. Even when you remain under the same roof for a time, the way bills are paid may become less straightforward.

Some expenses will be temporary. Others may be part of your new routine. It helps to distinguish between them. A moving truck is a one-time cost; rent is a continuing one. Replacing a bed may be urgent; buying a complete set of new furniture may not be.

You may also be dealing with uncertainty about who will pay particular bills while you separate. Do not assume that an arrangement you consider fair is necessarily the arrangement that will apply. Questions about property, debt, financial support, and obligations during separation depend on your circumstances and the law where you live. Your lawyer is the right person to explain those issues.

For now, start with the next month or two. Which bills are due? What money is available to pay them? Which expenses cannot wait? What information is missing? Those questions are manageable, even when the longer-term picture is not.

Four Groups of Numbers

It is useful to separate your finances into four groups: assets, debts, income, and expenses. They answer different questions, and combining them can make the situation look more confusing than it is.

Assets are things with financial value: bank balances, savings, investments, retirement accounts, property, vehicles, and valuable personal belongings. You may have an estimate rather than a confirmed value for some items. That is fine as a starting point, provided you label it clearly.

Debts are amounts owed: mortgages, credit cards, vehicle loans, student loans, personal loans, and other obligations. A loan balance is not the same thing as its monthly repayment. You will need both figures for different purposes.

Income is money coming in, such as wages, self-employment earnings, or other reliable payments. For budgeting, take-home pay is often more useful than gross salary. Be careful about treating uncertain future payments as money already available.

Expenses are the amounts you spend to live: housing, groceries, transportation, healthcare, insurance, childcare, and everything else that needs to be paid regularly. Some occur monthly; others arrive once or twice a year and are easy to forget.

Consider a couple who own a house with a mortgage. The house may be an asset, but that does not mean the entire estimated value is available to spend. The mortgage is a separate debt. Nor does the existence of equity mean there is cash in a checking account to cover next month's rent. Keeping these categories separate helps you see both the overall position and the immediate cash-flow problem.

What You Know, What You Think, and What You Need to Find Out

You may know the household finances very well. Or perhaps your spouse has always handled the accounts and you know little beyond the everyday bills. Many people fall somewhere in between. None of these starting points tells you whether you are capable of managing your finances now.

Take a sheet of paper and make three columns: **Confirmed**, **Estimated**, and **Unknown**. A current bank statement might belong in Confirmed. The likely value of your home might be Estimated. The balance of a retirement account you have never seen might be Unknown.

This simple distinction matters. An estimate is not a fact, and an unknown figure is not zero. When you speak to your lawyer or financial adviser, they can help you identify which missing numbers are important and how to obtain them appropriately.

Use the documents you collected in Chapter 4. Do not access private accounts, guess passwords, or take records you are not authorized to obtain. If information is controlled by your spouse, list what is missing and seek advice about the proper process for obtaining it. If you are concerned about monitoring or retaliation, get advice about a safe approach before searching for documents or changing financial arrangements.

Your Financial Starting Point

This worksheet is intended to give you a working overview, not a formal financial statement. Use approximate figures where necessary, mark them as estimates, and update them when better information becomes available.

Assets — approximate balances or values

Checking and savings accounts:	$____________________
Retirement accounts, including 401(k) and IRA accounts:	$____________________
Investments:	$____________________
Home and other real estate:	$____________________
Vehicles and valuable personal property:	$____________________
Business interests or other assets, if applicable:	$____________________

Debts — outstanding balances

Mortgage and home-equity loans: $________________

Auto, student, and personal loans: $________________

Credit cards: $________________

Business debts or other obligations: $________________

Monthly income — money you can reasonably count on

Take-home pay: $________________

Other regular income: $________________

Support payments currently being received: $________________

Other assistance or benefits, if applicable: $________________

Monthly expenses — current or anticipated

Rent or mortgage payment: $________________

Utilities, internet, and phone: $________________

Groceries and household supplies: $________________

Transportation, fuel, and insurance: $________________

Health insurance, prescriptions, and medical costs: $________________

Childcare, school, and children's activities: $________________

Minimum debt repayments: $__________________

Personal expenses and subscriptions: $__________________

Other essential expenses: $__________________

Allowance for less frequent expenses: $__________________

Total monthly income: **$__________________**

Total monthly expenses: **$__________________**

Difference (income minus expenses): **$__________________**

The difference is a starting point, not a verdict on your future. If the number is negative, it tells you there is a gap that needs attention. It does not tell you which legal arrangements will apply or what assistance might be available. Those are questions to investigate, not answers to invent.

Be careful not to count a debt repayment twice. The credit card balance belongs in your list of debts; the monthly amount you pay toward it belongs in your budget. Similarly, the value of your home belongs in the assets section, while your mortgage payment belongs among expenses.

Build Two Budgets, Not One

Your present household budget may be quite different from a budget for living separately. Rather than trying to make one set of figures cover both situations, create two versions.

The first shows **today**: the money currently available and the bills being paid. The second shows a **possible separate household**: expected rent, utilities, transportation, groceries, insurance, and other costs if you move. If the second budget contains guesses, mark them clearly.

For example, you may know your current mortgage payment but not the cost of renting nearby. Researching realistic rental prices can make the second budget more useful. You might also discover that a cheaper property would mean higher transportation or childcare costs. The cheapest single item is not always the cheapest overall arrangement.

Do not build a future budget around a property settlement, support payment, or sale of an asset that has not been agreed or confirmed. You can make a separate scenario showing what might change if a particular outcome occurs, but keep it distinct from the money you can rely on today.

If you have children, include the everyday costs of their care, not just the largest expenses. School lunches, uniforms, sports, medication, and transportation may be small individually but significant together. Some costs may change depending on where the children spend their time. Record your assumptions so you can revisit them.

Remember the Expenses That Do Not Arrive Every Month

Monthly budgets can be misleading because some bills are irregular. Car registration, insurance premiums, school supplies, holiday travel, home repairs, and medical costs may arrive only occasionally. They still need to be paid.

One way to account for them is to estimate the annual cost and divide it by twelve. If car insurance costs $1,200 a year, setting aside $100 a month makes the expense visible in your budget, even if the bill is not due yet. This does not mean you must immediately save that amount. It simply gives you a more realistic picture.

You may also need a short list of one-time separation costs: a rental deposit, moving expenses, replacing essential household items, or professional fees. Keep that list separate from your ordinary monthly spending. Otherwise, a particularly expensive month may make your ongoing budget look worse than it really is.

When the Numbers Do Not Add Up

Discovering that your anticipated expenses exceed your income can be frightening. It may be tempting to respond by making a quick decision: moving immediately, agreeing to a financial proposal, taking on a loan, or using retirement savings without understanding the consequences.

Try to identify the size and timing of the gap first. Is there enough to pay the bills due this week? What about next month? Which expenses are essential, and which can be delayed or reduced? Are there temporary arrangements you need to discuss with your lawyer? A financial professional may also help you compare options and understand their implications.

If you cannot cover immediate necessities, seek timely advice and ask about appropriate community or financial assistance. Do not wait for a complete divorce plan before addressing an urgent shortfall. Equally, avoid assuming that the first available borrowing option is the right one. Interest, fees, and repayment obligations can create a new problem later.

A budget is useful because it makes these questions visible. It cannot answer them all by itself.

Rachael and Bradley: Working Through the Figures

Rachael and Bradley have two daughters, Pippa, six, and Sally, eight. During much of their marriage, Rachael has managed the household and cared for the children while Bradley has earned most of the family's income. She knows what the groceries cost and when the school fees are due. Bradley has generally dealt with the mortgage, retirement savings, and investments.

When they begin discussing separation, Rachael initially assumes she can afford a small rental near the girls' school. She has looked at advertised rents and calculated what she spends on food and fuel. But when she sits down with the worksheet, she realizes she has left out health insurance, car maintenance, and several annual expenses. She also does not know what money, if any, will be available to her while longer-term arrangements are being considered.

Rachael starts by gathering the statements she can access and marking the missing figures. Her first budget has gaps, but it gives her something concrete to discuss. She asks her lawyer what questions need to be resolved before she signs a lease or agrees to a financial arrangement. She also meets with a financial adviser to compare different housing costs and consider what she could realistically manage each month.

The conversations do not produce an instant answer. Some figures depend on information Bradley has not yet provided, and some arrangements remain undecided. Rachael does, however, change her approach. Instead of asking only, "Can I afford this rent?" she asks, "What will my complete monthly costs be, what income can I rely on, and what needs to be confirmed before I commit?"

That is a more useful question. It does not guarantee a particular outcome, but it reduces the risk of making a decision with only half the information.

When to Ask for Financial Advice

A lawyer and a financial professional do different jobs. Your lawyer can explain legal rights, obligations, processes, and the questions that need to be considered under the law in your state. An accountant, financial adviser, or other appropriately qualified professional may help you understand budgets, taxes, retirement savings, borrowing, or the longer-term consequences of financial choices.

You may not need every adviser at once. Think about the questions that are causing the most uncertainty. Do you need help understanding a tax return? Are you considering whether to keep or sell a property? Are you unsure how a proposed arrangement would affect your monthly living costs? Those are useful reasons to seek targeted advice.

Before an appointment, take the figures you have, your list of missing information, and a few specific questions. You might ask:

- Which of my figures are reliable enough to plan around?
- What costs have I probably overlooked?
- How would this option affect my cash flow over the next six to twelve months?
- What tax, retirement, or borrowing issues should I ask a specialist about?
- Which decisions should wait until I have more information or legal advice?

If fees are a concern, ask what information the professional needs before the meeting and whether a focused consultation is possible. Preparing questions can help you use the time well.

A Small Financial Exercise

Choose one manageable task rather than trying to complete every worksheet in a sitting. You could list your accounts, total your essential monthly expenses, check the latest loan balances, or identify three figures you need to confirm.

Then write down **one decision you should not make yet**. Perhaps you are not ready to sign a lease, agree to take responsibility for a debt, or assume you can keep the family home. Record what information or advice would help you make that decision more carefully.

Return to your figures as circumstances change. A budget made before someone moves out may need updating afterwards. New information may alter your estimates. That is not evidence that the first exercise was wasted; it is how a working plan becomes more accurate.

Understanding your finances won't resolve every question, but it will help you recognize which decisions you can make now and which require further information or advice.

In the next chapter, we'll turn to the children: how to talk with them about separation, maintain familiar routines, and help them adjust to the changes around them.

Chapter 6: Protect Your Children

If you have children, separation involves decisions that reach well beyond the relationship between you and your spouse. You may be trying to work out where everyone will live, what to tell the children, how school mornings will work, and whether the arrangements you have in mind are realistic. At the same time, you may be carrying your own sadness, anger, or uncertainty.

You may want to protect your children from every difficult feeling, but separation will bring changes they may find upsetting. What matters is how you respond: paying attention to their needs, keeping adult problems with the adults, and making thoughtful decisions about the things within your control.

This chapter looks at how children may respond to separation, how to talk with them, and what practical support can look like in everyday life. It also recognizes that families are different. Advice about cooperative parenting must never override concerns about abuse, intimidation, or safety.

How Separation Can Affect Children

Children do not experience separation in one predictable way. One child may be upset about leaving a bedroom; another may worry about whether both parents will attend a school concert. A teenager might be angry about having to move between homes. A younger child might repeatedly ask whether the family will live together again. Some children feel relief when a tense household becomes calmer.

Siblings can respond differently even when they hear the same explanation and live through the same changes. Their age, personality, relationships, and previous experiences all matter. Responses may also change. A child who seems comfortable with a new routine in the first month may have questions several months later, when the reality of two homes feels more permanent.

A child's first reaction may not tell you everything about how they are coping. A child who seems untroubled may have worries they haven't expressed, while anger may reflect frustration about a particular change rather than the separation itself. Notice what they say, but also pay attention to changes in sleep, appetite, friendships, school participation, or behavior. If distress persists or affects daily life, ask a qualified professional for guidance rather than trying to diagnose the problem yourself.

Children also notice more than adults sometimes expect. They may hear an argument from another room, sense the tension after a difficult phone call, or understand that one parent is upset even when nobody explains why. This does not mean you have to pretend everything is fine. It means being careful about what you ask them to carry.

Keep Adult Conflict with the Adults

One of the most useful things you can do is keep children out of disputes about the separation. They do not need to know who said what in a legal appointment, why a bill was not paid, or which parent you believe is being unreasonable. Those matters may feel urgent to you, but they are not a child's responsibility.

This can be harder than it sounds. Imagine your child asks why their other parent has not collected them at the agreed time. You may know the reason, or you may be frustrated because it has happened before. A response such as "Your dad never thinks about anyone else" places an adult judgment in the child's hands. A steadier response is: "I know you were expecting to go. I'm checking what has happened, and I'll let you know what I find out."

You can acknowledge a disappointment without recruiting your child to your side. You can also set boundaries when they ask for details: "That's something the adults are working through. You don't have to solve it."

Avoid asking children to deliver messages, report on the other household, or keep secrets about adult arrangements. Even a seemingly small request—"Tell your mom she needs to answer my email"—can leave a child feeling responsible for communication between parents. Use a direct, appropriate method of communication instead, or seek advice about alternatives when direct contact is unsafe.

Children should not become your confidants. An older teenager may be thoughtful and caring, and it can be tempting to tell them how lonely or frightened you feel. But there is a difference between saying, "I'm having a difficult day, and I'm getting support," and relying on your child to comfort you or advise you about the marriage. Take those conversations to trusted adults or a professional.

When Safety Changes the Conversation

The advice to cooperate with the other parent assumes that cooperation is safe and appropriate. It may not be. If there has been family violence, coercive control, threats, stalking, or intimidation, ordinary suggestions about joint discussions and flexible communication can be unsuitable.

Children can be affected by frightening behavior even when they are not directly targeted. Their safety, and your own, come before creating the appearance of an amicable separation. If you are concerned, speak with a qualified local domestic violence service, lawyer, or other appropriate professional about safe communication, parenting arrangements, and practical steps. In immediate danger, contact emergency services.

Do not assume that a child should be encouraged into contact or joint family meetings without considering safety. Nor should you ask a child to investigate, document, or manage a parent's behavior. Adults and appropriately qualified professionals must handle those concerns.

What to Tell Your Children

Children generally need an explanation that is truthful, suited to their age, and focused on what affects them. They do not need a detailed account of the adult relationship. You may want to explain everything so they understand your decision, but too much information can leave them with questions they are not equipped to answer.

Where it is safe and realistic, parents may choose to agree on a simple message before speaking with their children. Where that is not possible, one parent can still communicate carefully. A useful starting point is: "We have decided that we will not live together anymore. This is an adult decision, and it is not because of anything you did. We are working out what will happen next. You can ask questions, and we will tell you what we know."

The details should reflect your circumstances. Do not say both parents will always be available or that nothing important will change if you cannot be sure. Children can manage an honest "We don't know yet" better than a promise that later proves untrue. If a decision about housing, school, or time with a parent has not been made, explain what is settled and what is still being worked out.

Consider the setting. Choose a time when you can give the conversation your attention, rather than announcing it on the way to school or immediately before bedtime. Leave room for questions, but do not expect an immediate response. A child may want to return to their game, ask for a snack, or change the subject. That does not mean the conversation failed.

You may need to have the same conversation more than once. Children often revisit questions as arrangements change or as they become old enough to understand more. A brief follow-up—"You've had a few days to think about what we said. Is there anything you're wondering about?"—can be more helpful than pressing for feelings on the first day.

Talking with Children at Different Ages

Younger children. Children in the early years often think in concrete terms. They may want to know where they will sleep, who will take them to school, and whether their toys or pets will move. Keep explanations short. Reassure them that the separation is not their fault, and repeat practical information as needed. Drawing, playing, or reading together may give them a comfortable way to raise questions.

School-aged children. Children in this group may ask more detailed questions or develop strong opinions about what should happen. Answer the question they have asked without giving them the full history of the marriage. If they say they want everything to go back to normal, acknowledge the wish rather than arguing them out of it.

Explain what is known about routines and when they can expect further information.

Teenagers. Teenagers may understand more about relationships and money, but that does not make them responsible for adult decisions. Respect their need for privacy, friendships, activities, and a voice about how changes affect them. Avoid asking them to choose sides or make decisions that belong to parents and professionals. Some may prefer to speak to a trusted relative, school counselor, or another adult rather than discussing every feeling with you.

These are broad guides, not rules. A child's development, temperament, disability, communication needs, and family circumstances may matter more than their age. Adapt your approach to the child in front of you.

Make Daily Life More Predictable

A separation can change the practical details that make a child's day feel familiar. There may be a new route to school, different meal times, unfamiliar rooms, or changes to after-school activities. You cannot always avoid disruption, particularly when money or housing is tight. You can still look for small points of continuity.

Keep a few ordinary routines where possible: a bedtime story, a regular call with a grandparent, soccer practice, a familiar breakfast, or the way you say goodnight. If a routine has to change, explain the change in advance when you can. Children may find a simple calendar helpful, especially once arrangements are confirmed and safe to share.

Try to separate what is important from what is merely familiar. A child may need predictable school pickups, but the exact dinner menu may not matter. Another child may be particularly attached to a weekly activity or a favorite object that moves between homes. Ask what helps rather than assuming you know.

Think about the practical problems before they become arguments. Who has the school uniform? Where is the medication? Who knows about the upcoming excursion? How will teachers be told about changes that affect pickup arrangements or a child's well-being? You do not need an elaborate system, but reliable information helps reduce avoidable stress.

If an arrangement is not working, review it. A schedule that looked sensible on paper may leave a child exhausted by long drives or constant packing. Noticing that problem is useful information, not evidence that you have failed.

Protect Your Relationship with Your Child

You may be worried that your relationship with your child will change when you no longer live together every day. It probably will change in some ways. That does not mean it must become less meaningful. Pay attention to the time you do have together and to how your child experiences it.

There is no need to turn every visit into a special occasion. Ordinary time matters: making dinner, helping with homework, going to the grocery store, or listening to a story about school. Children do not need competing holidays, gifts, or performances of happiness to know they are loved.

Listen when a child says something difficult. If they miss the other parent while they are with you, that is not necessarily a criticism. You might say, “Of course you miss them. Would it help to talk about that?” Where contact is safe and appropriate, support the relationships that matter to your child without asking them to reassure you that they love you too.

If a child raises a concern about their safety or treatment, take it seriously. Listen calmly, avoid coaching or interrogating them, and seek appropriate professional advice. Supporting a relationship with another parent should never require dismissing genuine safety concerns.

Activities That Make Room for Conversation

Not every child wants to sit down for a formal talk. Some open up while walking the dog, cooking, building something, or sitting in the car. A conversation that starts with school lunch may eventually reach a worry about the new house. Make yourself available without turning every quiet moment into a question about feelings.

For a younger child, you could invite them to draw the people and places that help them feel safe. A school-aged child might enjoy choosing a few familiar things to keep in each home, where possible. A teenager might prefer a notebook, private journal, or conversation with someone outside the immediate family. These are invitations, not assignments.

Books and stories about changing families can help children find words for experiences they have not yet described. Choose material that fits your child’s age and situation. A story can open a conversation, but you do not need to insist on a lesson at the end of it.

Be cautious about organizing joint family meetings simply because they sound constructive. Some families benefit from calm, child-focused conversations with both parents. Others do not, especially where conflict or intimidation makes those meetings distressing or unsafe. Use the approach that protects the child rather than the one that looks most cooperative from the outside.

Knowing When to Ask for Help

You are not expected to be a child psychologist. If your child seems persistently distressed, withdraws from usual activities, struggles significantly at school, or you are unsure how to respond, seek guidance from an appropriately qualified professional. A pediatrician, school counselor, or licensed child mental health professional may be able to help you identify the next step.

Professional support can also help parents. You may want advice about explaining a complicated change, responding to repeated questions, or managing communication with the other parent. A qualified professional can help you consider your child's particular circumstances and identify practical ways to respond.

If there are legal or safety concerns about parenting arrangements, speak with a qualified lawyer or appropriate local service. This book cannot tell you which arrangements are lawful or suitable for your particular family.

A Practical Check-In

Before you move on, think about each child separately. What has changed for them recently? What has stayed familiar? What have they asked about, and what have you not yet been able to answer? Is there one practical change—such as a clearer pickup plan, a conversation with a teacher, or time with a trusted adult—that might make the coming week easier?

Then consider your own behavior. Have you asked a child to carry a message, take sides, or reassure you about an adult worry? If so, you can change course. You do not need to make a speech about it. A simple acknowledgment—"I shouldn't have put you in the middle of that. I'll handle it"—can matter.

Children need adults to take responsibility for adult decisions, explain changes in ways they can understand, and notice when additional support is needed. Much of that happens in ordinary moments: a conversation after school, a familiar routine, or a question answered with care.

Chapter 7: Communicate Well

There may be conversations you would rather not have. Who will collect the children on Friday? What happens to the mortgage payment next month? When can you collect your belongings? Even when both people accept that the relationship is ending, the ordinary details still have to be discussed.

Communication can make those details easier to manage. It can also become one of the most exhausting parts of separation. A question about a utility bill may turn into an argument about the marriage. A reasonable request may receive no answer. You may find yourself rewriting a message five times, trying to avoid a reaction you cannot predict.

Good communication is not a guarantee of agreement. It is a way of making your position understandable, getting the information you need, and recognizing when a conversation is no longer useful. You can take responsibility for how you communicate. You cannot take responsibility for the other person's response.

This chapter is about practical communication: deciding what needs discussing, choosing a suitable method, listening without surrendering your position, and knowing when professional help or distance is the better option.

Start with the Purpose of the Conversation

Before contacting your spouse or former spouse, ask yourself what you need from the exchange. Are you sharing information, asking a question, making a proposal, or trying to reach a decision? Those are different tasks. A message that tries to do all four may be difficult to answer.

For example, you might need to confirm who is paying the electricity bill. That is a specific practical question. It does not require a conversation about which of you contributed more to the household over the last ten years. Those feelings may be real and important, but they are unlikely to help you decide what happens before Friday.

A useful starting point is to write the purpose in one sentence: "I need to confirm the children's pickup arrangements for next week." If you cannot do that, you may need to separate several issues or gather more information first.

It also helps to distinguish an urgent issue from an uncomfortable one. A bill due tomorrow or a change to a child's medication may need prompt attention. A proposal about selling the house may be important without requiring an answer that evening. Allowing time to think can protect you from decisions made simply to end a difficult exchange.

Choose the Method That Works

Face-to-face conversation is not automatically the best option. Some people communicate calmly in person but struggle by text. Others find a written message easier because they can think before responding and keep track of what has been said.

A phone call may be useful for a straightforward question that needs a quick answer. Email may suit a more complicated issue, particularly if you need to attach documents or set out options. A shared calendar or other agreed tool can help with routine arrangements, provided it is appropriate and safe for your circumstances.

Think about privacy as well. A conversation in a crowded cafe may not be suitable for sensitive financial information. A discussion during school pickup can expose children to tension or adult details. A message sent to a shared email account may not be private. If you have concerns about access to your devices or accounts, seek specialist advice about safer communication.

You can suggest a different method without making it a personal criticism: "I'd prefer to deal with the school schedule by email so we can both check the dates." That is clearer than "You always twist what I say."

Where there has been abuse, intimidation, stalking, coercive control, or threats, direct communication may be unsafe. Suggestions about calm discussion, joint meetings, and compromise do not apply in the same way. Ask a qualified local lawyer or specialist domestic violence service about appropriate channels and safety planning. In immediate danger, contact emergency services.

Prepare Before You Begin

Before a difficult conversation, identify the issue, the information you already have, and anything you need to check. You don't need to anticipate every objection or prepare a response to every possible argument.

Imagine you want to discuss the children's school vacation. Look at the dates before you start. Consider your work commitments, travel plans, and any existing arrangements. Think about what would work for the children rather than beginning with a demand for a particular number of days. If legal arrangements or safety concerns affect the discussion, obtain advice before proposing changes.

You might make a short note with three headings: what is known, what needs to be decided, and what requires advice. This can be particularly useful when a conversation becomes emotional. You can return to the question instead of trying to resolve the entire relationship in one sitting.

Consider timing. Starting a major discussion late at night, immediately after an argument, or while either of you is rushing may make a hard conversation harder. You may be able to say, "This matters, and I want to give it proper attention. Can we exchange our thoughts tomorrow?" If a response is genuinely urgent, explain the deadline and why it matters.

Listening Without Agreeing

Listening carefully does not mean accepting the other person's account of events. You can understand their concern and still disagree with the solution they propose.

Suppose your former spouse says they cannot manage a particular pickup because of work. You might respond, "I understand that your shift finishes at six. The children need to be collected at three, so we still need another arrangement." You have acknowledged the information without accepting responsibility for solving the problem alone.

Ask questions when the answer is unclear. "Are you saying you can do Thursday instead?" is more helpful than assuming a refusal means the other person does not care. Equally, do not feel obliged to keep asking when someone is deliberately avoiding the question or using the exchange to intimidate you.

Try to avoid building an argument around what you believe the other person meant. You may know their habits very well, but a message can still be ambiguous. Check the practical point when it is safe to do so. A neutral question can save several rounds of misunderstanding.

Say What You Need to Say

Clear language is often more useful than perfect language. You do not need a special formula to make a difficult conversation successful.

"I" statements can help when they identify a practical need: "I need the pickup time confirmed by Thursday so I can arrange work." They are less useful when they disguise an accusation: "I feel that you are completely irresponsible." The distinction is not grammatical; it is about whether the sentence gives the other person something specific to respond to.

Keep requests manageable. "Can you send me the insurance details by Monday?" is easier to answer than a long message about every document that has not yet been provided. If there are several questions, number them or separate them into messages when appropriate.

Be careful about explanations that are really attempts to persuade someone to agree with your entire version of the marriage. You may want your former spouse to understand why you are hurt. That desire is understandable. But if the immediate issue is a school form or a bank statement, you may not get the emotional acknowledgment you want from that conversation. Trusted friends, a counselor, or another suitable professional may be better placed to help you process those feelings.

When the Conversation Becomes Difficult

A discussion can begin reasonably and still go off course. Voices rise, old grievances appear, or one person insists on an immediate answer. Notice the change rather than treating it as something you must push through.

You can pause without abandoning the issue: "We're not making progress on this tonight. I'll put my questions in an email tomorrow." If you need advice, say so: "I understand the proposal, but I won't agree to it until I've spoken with my lawyer." Those statements are not threats. They explain the next step.

Avoid making financial, parenting, or property commitments just to stop an argument. A quick agreement may create practical problems later, and some arrangements may have legal consequences. If you are unsure, take time to obtain advice from an appropriately qualified professional in your state.

Sometimes the other person will not respect a pause or boundary. Repeating your explanation may not help. You may need to end the exchange and use another channel. If you feel threatened or unsafe, prioritize safety and seek appropriate support rather than attempting to improve the tone of the conversation.

Working Toward Agreements

Where discussion is safe and appropriate, an agreement often begins with a shared understanding of the question. What exactly is being decided? What information is missing? What options are available? Who needs to do what next?

Consider a conversation about the family home. One person may want to sell immediately; the other may hope to stay. Before arguing about the final outcome, you might need to establish the mortgage balance, ongoing costs, housing alternatives, and what legal or financial advice each person requires. Identifying those steps is progress even if you have not reached an agreement.

It can help to separate temporary arrangements from final decisions. You may be able to agree about who will pay a particular bill this month while leaving the longer-term financial arrangements for professional advice. Make sure you understand the implications before relying on any temporary understanding, and do not assume that an informal exchange is legally binding.

If you do reach a practical understanding, record it accurately. A brief follow-up might say: "My understanding is that you will collect the children on Tuesday at four, and we'll discuss the following week once the work roster is available." Invite corrections rather than declaring a disputed conversation settled. For legal arrangements, ask your lawyer what documentation or formal steps are required.

A Worked Example: The School Vacation

Imagine that you and your former spouse both want time with the children during the winter school vacation. You receive a message saying, "I'm taking them for the first week. You can have the second." You had hoped to take them away during the first week, and your immediate reaction is frustration.

Before responding, check the dates and any existing arrangements. Ask yourself whether the proposal is a request, an assumption, or a decision already made. You might write: "I haven't agreed to those dates. I was hoping to travel with the children during the first week. Could we look at the calendar and consider the options?"

If the other parent replies that their work leave is already approved, you have new information. You still do not have to agree immediately. You might ask whether dates can be adjusted or whether another arrangement is possible. If discussions become circular, suggest exchanging written proposals or seeking appropriate professional assistance.

The goal is not to produce the perfect message. It is to avoid turning a scheduling question into a competition about which parent cares more. It is also to recognize when you need advice about existing parenting arrangements rather than trying to negotiate around them yourself.

A Practical Guide to Difficult Conversations

Use these questions before a discussion or written exchange. They are prompts, not a script you must follow.

1. **What is the issue?** Write down the one decision or piece of information you need. If several issues are tangled together, decide which one should come first.

2. **What do I know?** Identify the relevant dates, documents, costs, or existing arrangements. Note what you still need to confirm.

3. **What matters most?** Think about practical needs, children's routines, safety, and any limits on what you can agree to. Not every preference has the same importance.

4. **What options could work?** Consider more than one possibility when it is safe and reasonable. You do not have to offer a concession simply to appear cooperative.

5. **What requires advice?** Identify proposals involving legal rights, significant money, parenting arrangements, or safety concerns that you should discuss with a qualified professional before agreeing.

6. **How will I communicate?** Choose an appropriate time and method. Decide whether direct contact is suitable at all.

7. **What happens next?** Record what was decided, what remains open, and who will follow up. If no agreement was reached, that can be recorded plainly too.

For a routine question, a short message may be enough: "The dentist has offered appointments on Tuesday and Thursday. Which works with your schedule?" For a larger issue, it may be better to say: "I have some questions about the house and would like to get advice before we discuss a decision."

When Talking Is Not Enough

Some issues are too complicated, contentious, or sensitive to resolve in direct conversation. A lawyer can help you understand your options and what information you need. Mediation or another structured process may be helpful in suitable circumstances, but it is not appropriate in every case. Where there are safety concerns or a significant imbalance of power, ask about safer alternatives and professional safeguards.

Professional assistance can take some of the pressure out of difficult exchanges. You can remain courteous while asking that significant proposals go through your lawyer, or decide that direct communication is inappropriate where safety is a concern.

Some conversations will go better than others. What matters is whether you communicated clearly, considered the consequences of any commitments, and paid attention to safety.

Sometimes that will mean a thoughtful discussion. Sometimes it will mean a short, factual email. And sometimes the most sensible decision will be to let a professional handle the conversation.

Chapter 8: Build a Support Network

Separation can make an ordinary week surprisingly complicated. You may be organizing new living arrangements, collecting documents, speaking with professionals, answering messages, and trying to keep work and family life moving. The practical tasks do not stop because you are having a difficult day.

There may also be a strange loneliness to it. Even if friends know you are separating, they may not know what to say. Some will offer help immediately. Others may stay quiet because they do not want to intrude. You might find yourself explaining the same thing several times, or deciding you would rather explain nothing at all.

A support network is not a committee that needs to know every detail of your marriage. It is a small collection of people and services who can help with different things. Some may listen. Some may help you get through a busy Thursday. Others may offer professional advice you cannot reasonably expect from a friend.

What matters is knowing who you can turn to, and for what.

Work Out What Kind of Help You Need

When someone says, “Let me know if you need anything,” it can be surprisingly hard to answer. You may not know what you need, or you may feel uncomfortable asking. A useful first step is to separate emotional support from practical help and professional advice.

Emotional support might mean having someone listen without trying to solve the problem. You might want company on a quiet evening, a walk with a friend, or someone who can hear that you had a bad day without turning it into a discussion about your former spouse.

Practical help is often less dramatic but just as valuable. It could be collecting children from school, bringing a meal, helping you move boxes, or sitting nearby while you organize paperwork. Sometimes the most helpful person is the one who can take one ordinary task off your list.

Professional support serves a different purpose. You may need a lawyer to explain your options, a financial adviser to help you understand a decision, or a counselor to talk through difficult feelings. Being clear about those different roles helps you ask the right person the right question.

Look at the next two weeks rather than the next two years. Is there an appointment you are anxious about? A childcare problem? A day when you expect to be particularly tired? You may find one specific request easier to make than a broad appeal for help.

For example: "Could you collect the children on Tuesday while I attend an appointment?" Or: "I don't need advice, but would you have time for a coffee this weekend?" Both requests give the other person something understandable to respond to.

Choose People Who Are Right for the Job

Not everyone who cares about you will be helpful in the same way. One friend may be wonderfully practical but uncomfortable talking about feelings. Another may be an excellent listener who immediately wants to tell you what to do. A relative may love you dearly but have strong opinions about whether the marriage should end.

Consider how you usually feel after speaking with someone. Do you feel heard? Can you trust them with private information? Will they respect decisions they might not make themselves?

Someone can care about you without being the right person to discuss every aspect of your separation.

It can help to have more than one person to turn to. If one friend is your only sounding board, every worry may end up in the same conversation. A small circle allows different people to help in ways that suit them and gives you some choice about what you share.

Be especially thoughtful about people who know both you and your spouse. Mutual friends may want to maintain relationships with both of you. They may feel caught in the middle, even when you have not asked them to take sides. You can ask for discretion, but you cannot control what another person repeats. Share sensitive information with that reality in mind.

You do not need to provide an explanation of the marriage to justify your decision to separate. "We're separating, and I'm not ready to discuss the details" is a complete answer. If you want to say more later, you can.

When Friends and Family Have Opinions

People often offer advice because they care. Unfortunately, caring does not make their advice right for your circumstances.

Someone may tell you to move out immediately, demand a particular financial outcome, or refuse to speak to your former spouse. Another may insist that you reconcile. People may draw on their own divorce experiences and assume yours will unfold in the same way.

You can listen without treating an opinion as an instruction. A simple response might be: “I know you’re looking out for me. I’m getting advice about that before I decide.” You do not have to debate the point or defend every choice.

If a conversation repeatedly leaves you distressed or pressured, consider changing what you discuss with that person. Perhaps they can help with groceries or keep you company at a movie, but they are not the person to talk to about parenting arrangements. Relationships can remain valuable even when you put boundaries around a particular subject.

Children also need protection from adult conversations. Be careful about asking relatives or friends to pass messages, collect information about your former spouse, or discuss disagreements in front of children. Someone can support you without becoming involved in the conflict.

Finding Support Beyond Your Usual Circle

Separation can change social routines. You may no longer feel comfortable attending certain gatherings, or you may discover that much of your social life was organized around being a couple. That can be unsettling, even if ending the marriage is the right decision for you.

You do not have to replace your entire social life at once. Consider one ordinary connection you can maintain: a weekly walk, a class, a book club, a colleague you enjoy having lunch with. Not every conversation needs to be about divorce. Time spent doing something familiar can be a welcome reminder that your life contains more than the separation.

Some people find divorce or separation support groups helpful. They can offer an opportunity to speak with others who recognize the practical and emotional difficulties involved. Groups may meet in person or online, and some are led by trained professionals.

Choose carefully. Look for respectful moderation, clear privacy expectations, and a culture that allows different experiences. Be cautious with groups that encourage hostility toward former spouses or present one member's legal outcome as a model everyone should follow. Divorce law and individual circumstances vary widely, particularly across US states.

Online spaces deserve particular care. A private group may not be as private as it appears. Screenshots can be shared, and posts can remain accessible long after you have changed your mind about what you wanted to disclose. Avoid posting confidential documents, identifying details about children, or information that could compromise your safety. If you are unsure about sharing something relevant to legal proceedings, ask your lawyer first.

Knowing When Professional Help Would Be Useful

Friends and family can be generous and thoughtful, but they cannot reasonably do everything. You may find yourself asking a friend to interpret a legal letter, or expecting your lawyer to help you process an argument that happened the night before. Those are understandable impulses when so many issues overlap.

Try to match the question to the professional. A lawyer can advise on legal rights, responsibilities, processes, and the implications of a proposed arrangement in your state. A qualified financial professional may help with budgets, taxes, long-term planning, or questions about financial products. A counselor, therapist, or other appropriately qualified mental health professional can help you work through distress, conflict, or changes in your relationships.

You do not need to be in crisis to seek counseling. You may simply want a confidential place to talk where the other person has no connection to your marriage. Equally, counseling is not a requirement for getting through separation. Some people rely mainly on friends and practical routines; others find regular professional conversations useful.

If money is tight, ask about costs before booking. You can enquire about community services, employee assistance programs, local nonprofit organizations, or providers offering reduced fees. Availability and eligibility differ, so check what is offered in your area rather than assuming a particular service will be accessible.

If you are already working with a professional, be clear about what you want from the appointment. You might say to a counselor, "I'm having trouble sleeping before conversations about the children," or to your lawyer, "I need to know whether I should agree to this proposed arrangement." A specific question can make the time more useful.

Pay Attention to How You Are Coping

Friends and family may be able to listen, offer reassurance, or help with practical tasks. Sometimes, however, the difficulties you are experiencing call for professional support.

If distress is persistent, your sleep is seriously disrupted, or you are finding it difficult to manage ordinary responsibilities, consider speaking with a qualified health professional. You do not need to diagnose what is happening or wait until the situation becomes unmanageable before seeking advice.

Having a mental health condition does not automatically mean someone cannot parent well or make thoughtful decisions. If a health issue raises a specific legal question in your circumstances, speak with your own lawyer.

If you have immediate concerns about your safety or thoughts of harming yourself, seek urgent local crisis or emergency assistance.

Where there has been abuse, intimidation, stalking, or coercive control, ordinary suggestions about leaning on mutual friends or communicating openly may not be safe. Consider whether someone has access to your accounts, location, messages, or devices before contacting services or sharing plans. A specialist domestic violence organization or appropriately qualified local professional can help you consider safer options. In immediate danger, contact emergency services.

A Story About Asking for Help

Imagine that Maya has recently separated. She works full time and has two school-aged children. Her sister lives nearby and keeps asking what she can do, but Maya always replies that she is fine. Meanwhile, she is trying to schedule a legal appointment, organize bank statements, and manage a change to the children's after-school activities.

One evening Maya realizes she has spent an hour worrying about how to fit everything into Thursday. She calls her sister and asks whether she could collect the children that afternoon. Her sister agrees immediately. Maya then asks a trusted friend if they could meet for coffee over the weekend. She tells the friend she would rather talk about how she is feeling than receive advice about the divorce.

Neither conversation resolves the separation. The legal questions remain, and Maya still has paperwork to do. But Thursday is manageable, and she has somewhere to take the feelings that have been accumulating. She has not handed over her decisions. She has simply allowed other people to help with parts of a difficult week.

That is often what a useful support network looks like. It does not need to be impressive or large. It needs to work in real life.

A Check-In: Who Is in Your Corner?

You can use these prompts now and revisit them as your circumstances change. Write down names if that helps, but do not worry about filling every space.

Someone who listens: Who can hear how I am feeling without judging me or passing on private details?

Someone practical: Who could help with a specific task, appointment, meal, or childcare arrangement?

Someone outside the situation: Is there a friend, group, or professional who is not connected to my former spouse?

Professional questions: What should I take to my lawyer, financial adviser, doctor, or counselor rather than asking friends to answer?

Privacy and safety: Who needs to know what is happening? Are there people or communication methods I should avoid?

My next request: What is one small, specific thing I could ask someone to help with this week?

The people you turn to may change as your circumstances change. Someone who helps you move house may not be the person you want to talk to six months later.

Start with one specific request. It might be help with the children, company after an appointment, or ten minutes with someone who will listen without offering advice.

You can keep your private life private and still let people help.

Chapter 9: Look After You

There is a particular kind of tiredness that can come with separation. You may be doing all the things you usually do—working, making dinner, getting children to school—while also managing appointments, paperwork, new arrangements, and conversations you would rather not have. Even a quiet day can leave you exhausted.

When so much needs attention, looking after yourself can seem like the least urgent item on the list. It is easy to decide you will sleep properly once the documents are organized, or take a day off when the arrangements are settled. But separation rarely offers a convenient moment when everything else stops.

This chapter is not an invitation to add an elaborate wellness routine to an already crowded week. It is about noticing what you need, protecting some of your capacity to make decisions, and finding a few habits that fit your actual circumstances.

What Self-Care Means in Real Life

Self-care has become a phrase that can mean almost anything. Sometimes it is associated with treats, retreats, or finding an hour of peace in a busy day. Those things can be lovely. They are not always available, and they are not the whole story.

During separation, self-care might mean making a doctor's appointment you have been postponing. It might mean eating lunch before a meeting with your lawyer, arranging someone to collect the children, or switching off your phone after a difficult exchange. It might mean asking your employer whether you can adjust your hours temporarily. None of these choices is especially glamorous. All may make a demanding week more manageable.

You may have limited money, limited time, or very little privacy. Perhaps you are living in the same home as your former spouse while working out the next steps. Perhaps you are now doing the work of two adults in one household. Advice that assumes you have spare hours and a generous budget will not be very helpful.

Start with the question: What would make tomorrow a little easier? The answer may be much smaller than you expect.

Pay Attention to the Basics

Stress can show up in ordinary ways. You might sleep lightly, lose your appetite, eat whatever is convenient, or forget something you would usually remember. You may find it difficult to concentrate on a document, even though you can manage your usual work perfectly well. People respond differently, and none of these experiences is a test of whether you are coping successfully.

Food, rest, hydration, and movement are not cures for the emotional and practical difficulties of divorce. They are basic needs worth protecting while you deal with those difficulties. If cooking feels like too much, simple meals are fine. If you cannot manage your usual exercise, a short walk or some gentle movement may be enough for now. If sleep is difficult, consider whether late-night messages, paperwork, or scrolling are making it harder to wind down.

Try to notice patterns rather than judging individual days. Are you regularly missing meals because appointments run late? Do conversations with your former spouse leave you awake for hours? Is there one recurring part of your week that could be rearranged or shared with someone else?

Persistent sleep problems, troubling physical symptoms, or changes in mood and functioning deserve attention from a qualified health professional. Do not assume every symptom is simply part of separation. Getting appropriate advice is a form of looking after yourself, too.

Movement Without Another Set of Rules

Exercise can be helpful during stressful periods, but it is easy to turn it into another obligation. A rigid routine may not be realistic when your days are already crowded with work, family responsibilities, and separation arrangements.

If you already have an activity you enjoy, consider how to keep it in your week. You might walk with a neighbor, swim, garden, stretch, or go to a class. Familiar activities can provide structure as well as a change of scene. If you have not exercised for a while, start gently and seek medical advice if you have health concerns or are unsure what is appropriate.

Movement need not be a project. Ten minutes outside between appointments may be more realistic than promising yourself an hour at the gym every morning. You can also build small pauses into the day: stand up after sorting documents, walk around the block before answering a difficult email, or take the longer route home if it gives you a moment to think.

The point is not to become fitter as proof that you are doing divorce well. It is to make room for an activity that feels manageable and, ideally, pleasant.

Give Your Mind Somewhere to Rest

There can be a lot of thinking involved in separation. You may rehearse conversations, imagine possible outcomes, revisit old arguments, and wonder what you have forgotten. Even when you are not actively doing anything about the divorce, it may occupy a great deal of mental space.

Some people find writing useful. You might keep one notebook for practical questions and another place for thoughts you do not need to act on. Others prefer reading, knitting, cooking, listening to music, sitting outside, or spending time with someone who does not want to discuss the separation at all.

If you enjoy breathing exercises, meditation, or yoga, they may be part of your routine. They are options, not requirements. You do not need to sit quietly with every difficult thought, and you do not need to turn each emotion into a lesson.

It can help to distinguish a problem you can act on from a worry you cannot resolve tonight. If you remember a question for your lawyer at 10 p.m., write it down. Unless it is urgent, you can deal with it during working hours. The note is there so you do not have to keep holding the question in your head.

Make Decisions When You Can Give Them Attention

Looking after yourself is also connected to the way you make decisions. A separation can produce a steady stream of requests: sign this, answer that, agree to a date, respond to a proposal. Some matters really do have deadlines. Others feel urgent because someone wants an answer immediately.

Before responding, ask what the decision involves, when an answer is genuinely required, and whether you have the information you need. You may want legal or financial advice before agreeing to something with lasting consequences. A short response—"I've received this and will reply after I've had a chance to consider it"—can be more useful than an answer made while upset or exhausted.

Notice the circumstances in which you tend to make rushed choices. Perhaps you reply to messages late at night because that is the only quiet time. Perhaps you agree to things during a tense conversation just to end it. If so, consider changing the process rather than relying on willpower. Use written communication where appropriate, set a time to review proposals, or ask your lawyer to handle a particular issue.

You won't always have the luxury of making decisions when you're rested and calm. But where circumstances allow, give yourself time to consider the information and consequences before responding. If there are immediate safety concerns, seek appropriate help rather than waiting.

Set Boundaries Around Separation Tasks

Divorce can expand to fill every available hour. There are always more documents to find, questions to research, and possible scenarios to consider. You may feel that if you stop thinking about it, you will miss something important.

Consider giving practical tasks a place in your week. You might set aside time on two evenings to organize paperwork or keep a running list of questions for professional appointments. If you have a deadline, work backwards from it and decide what must happen first. The aim is not a perfect schedule; it is to stop every spare moment becoming divorce administration.

Boundaries with other people may matter as well. You do not have to take every call immediately or discuss the separation with every curious acquaintance. You can tell a friend you would like to talk about something else for a while. You can decide that a particular family member is not the right person to discuss legal negotiations with.

Where there has been abuse, stalking, coercive control, or intimidation, ordinary advice about setting boundaries may be inadequate or unsafe. Seek guidance from an appropriate local specialist about communication, devices, and safety planning. Your safety matters more than maintaining a polite routine.

When You Have Children or People Depending on You

Parents often find that their own needs disappear behind the children's. There are school routines to protect, questions to answer, and perhaps new living arrangements to manage. You may feel guilty taking time for yourself when your children are unsettled.

Looking after yourself does not require withdrawing from your responsibilities. It may mean arranging a reliable babysitter for an appointment, accepting help with a school pickup, or preparing simple meals during a demanding week. If children are old enough, ordinary age-appropriate household tasks can continue, but they should not be asked to manage your emotions or become your main source of support.

The same applies if you are caring for an older parent or another family member. You may need to review what is realistic, at least temporarily. In Chapter 8, we considered the people who might help. Here, the question is whether you will allow yourself to use that help.

An Ordinary Week: Nina's Example

Imagine Nina has recently separated and is managing work and two children's schedules. She tells herself that once the next appointment is over, she will take better care of herself. But there is always another appointment. She has been answering messages after midnight and skipping lunch because she is trying to get everything done.

Nina does not need an ambitious new routine. She starts by putting a sandwich and water in her bag before leaving home. She asks her brother to collect the children on the afternoon of her legal appointment. She keeps a notebook by the bed so she can write down questions instead of searching for answers on her phone late at night.

Some days the plan falls apart. A child gets sick, work runs late, and Nina answers an upsetting message when she had intended to wait. The following week, she makes a few adjustments and keeps the parts of her routine that were useful.

Her circumstances have not suddenly become easy. But she has stopped treating her own needs as something to attend to only after everyone else's problems are solved.

A Practical Check-In

Rather than making a long list of habits to adopt, take a few minutes to answer these questions. You can write your answers down or simply think about them.

The basics: Have I been eating, resting, and sleeping as well as I reasonably can? Is there a health concern I should discuss with a professional?

My week: What is making this week especially difficult? Is there one task I could postpone, simplify, or ask someone else to do?

My decisions: Is there a decision I am trying to make without enough information? Who could help me understand it?

My boundaries: Is there a conversation, message thread, or habit that is taking more time and energy than it needs to?

Something for me: What is one ordinary activity I would like to keep in my life this week?

Choose one action you can realistically take in the next few days. You might book an appointment, prepare an easy dinner, ask a friend for help, or put aside an hour for something you enjoy. Choose something that will make a practical difference to your week.

When Things Do Not Go to Plan

There will be weeks when you do not manage any of this particularly well. You may forget lunch, cancel a walk, lose your temper, or spend an evening worrying about something that cannot yet be resolved. That does not undo the effort you have made.

If your plan is too difficult to maintain, make it smaller. If you need more help than friends can provide, speak with an appropriately qualified professional. If you feel persistently overwhelmed or unable to manage ordinary responsibilities, take that seriously and seek support. You do not need to wait until a crisis to ask.

Separation asks a lot of you, and much of it is outside your control. You may not be able to make the process simple or predictable. You can, however, notice when you need a break, ask a question before making a decision, and allow some room for ordinary life alongside the difficult parts.

The paperwork and decisions matter. So do you.

Conclusion

A separation involves more decisions than most people expect. Some are large and obvious: where to live, how to manage the money, what arrangements to make for children. Others are smaller, but still matter: which documents to find, what to say in a difficult conversation, and who to call when you need an answer rather than another opinion.

You may have reached the end of this book with a clearer picture of what lies ahead. You may also have a longer list of questions than when you started. That is not necessarily a bad thing. A useful question can prevent an expensive assumption, an unnecessary argument, or a decision made before you have the information you need.

The aim was never to show you how to have a perfect divorce. There is no reliable formula for one. A good divorce, as I have used the term here, is not measured by whether you remain friends, agree about everything, or avoid every difficult feeling. It is about approaching the decisions you can influence with care, obtaining sound advice, and reducing avoidable harm wherever possible. In some circumstances, particularly where there is abuse or intimidation, that may mean keeping your distance and asking professionals to help you manage the process safely.

What you now have to work with

Throughout this book, we have looked at the decisions, information, and arrangements that can make separation more manageable. Some of that work involves practical preparation: seeking legal advice, making a plan, gathering financial records, and understanding your household expenses. Other parts involve the people affected by those decisions: your children, your spouse, the people who support you, and yourself.

These matters are connected. A clearer financial picture may change your housing plans. Legal advice may help you recognize which arrangements should remain temporary. A difficult conversation may reveal that you need more information before making a commitment. And the support you have around you can affect how much time and attention you can give to the decisions ahead.

You may already have some of the information you need. Other questions will take longer to answer. The important thing is to distinguish between what you know, what you are assuming, and what requires further advice.

Turn the information into a next step

Take a fresh page and make three short lists:

1. What needs attention now.
2. What needs more information.
3. What can wait.

Try to be specific. "Sort out the finances" is a daunting task. "Find the last three bank statements and write down the monthly mortgage payment" is something you can begin.

Look at the first list and choose one or two actions that are realistic in the next few days. Perhaps you need to arrange an initial legal appointment. Perhaps you need to ask about a safe place to stay, establish how much money is available for immediate expenses, or talk with your children about a change that is already happening. Perhaps the next step is simply to sleep on a decision before making a promise you are not ready to keep.

For each action, ask yourself: Do I have the information I need? Is there anyone qualified who should advise me first? Could this affect my safety, my children, or my financial position? If the answer is uncertain, that is a reason to ask another question, not a reason to rush.

Keep your notes somewhere private and secure. Return to them as circumstances change. Cross things off when they are done. Add new questions when they arise.

There is no single way through

Some separations are cooperative. Others are not. Some people have savings, family nearby, and flexible work. Others are dealing with limited money, complicated housing arrangements, health concerns, or a spouse who will not engage constructively. The decisions that make sense for one family may be impractical or unsafe for another.

Progress may also be uneven. A productive meeting might be followed by a difficult weekend. A practical agreement might leave you unexpectedly sad. Or you may feel relief after resolving something that has worried you for months. None of those reactions changes the value of the practical work you have done.

Return to the information you have, the questions that remain, and the decision in front of you. Seek professional advice where it is needed. Give yourself time where circumstances allow. And remember that a plan can change as your circumstances become clearer.

Being informed does not mean knowing everything in advance. It means understanding what you can, recognizing what you do not yet know, and seeking help where it matters.

That is enough to begin with. One question, one conversation, one considered decision at a time.

Emily

About the Author

Emily R. Sterling writes about separation, divorce, difficult relationships, and the process of rebuilding life after significant change.

Writing under a pen name, Emily draws on extensive experience in family law, studies in psychology, and a longstanding curiosity about human behavior and relationships. Her writing reflects an appreciation of the complexities of relationships, the challenges people face when those relationships end, and the importance of understanding both the practical and emotional dimensions of separation.

Emily believes that knowledge, preparation, and perspective can make an enormous difference during life's most challenging transitions. Whether navigating a difficult separation, recognizing unhealthy relationship dynamics, or finding the confidence to begin again, her books offer practical guidance, thoughtful perspectives, and encouragement to make informed decisions.

Through *Break Free*, *Moving On*, and *Informed Separation*, Emily explores the challenges of ending relationships and the possibilities that lie beyond them.

At the heart of her writing is a simple belief: people deserve the information, perspective, and support to make their own decisions about what comes next.

Made in United States
North Haven, CT
10 November 2026

22088279R00065